"I was glad when they said unto me, Let us go into the house of the Lord."

Houses of Worship

by Patricia A. Pingry

An *ideals* Publication

ISBN 0-89542-053-8

© 1977 by Ideals Publishing Corporation
All rights reserved

Printed in the United States of America

Published by Ideals Publishing Corporation
11315 Watertown Plank Road
Milwaukee, Wis. 53266

Managing Editor, Ralph Luedtke
Photographic Editor, Gerald Koser
Production Editor, Stuart L. Zyduck

Designed by Patricia A. Pingry

Preface

This is not a book about religion. It is, instead, a book about churches, the buildings themselves, their purpose, their construction, and the people who raised them and worship in them. This is a look at those people who built God's houses, fought for the freedom to worship in them, and continue even now, building new churches and devising new religions.

Throughout its history, America has welcomed and embraced peoples from all countries, of all faiths. Each group who came brought its religion. One of the first tasks facing each group of settlers was building a church, a temple or a meeting house in which to practice their belief, thereby giving this country a religious heritage unequaled by the rest of the world.

Today, America has, perhaps, the grandest and costliest churches anywhere in the world. From the first crude shelters to the grand edifices of today, however, the purpose has remained the same: that of Glory to God.

St. Patrick's Cathedral
New York City

Contents

Mission bells of San
Juan Capistrano

Ed Cooper

"Wee shall be as a Citty vpon a Hill, the eies of all people are vppon vs . . ."

John Winthrop

Planting the Faith

The beginning of the New World was the arrival of settlers who brought their faith and whose first thought, upon setting foot upon the land, was to build a house where they might worship God. In the Northeast, the nonconformists came to build what John Winthrop called a "Citty vpon a Hill . . . for Gods sake" and sought a life free from religious persecution.

In the southern region, the planters came; and they, too, brought their faith. In Virginia, these farmers erected the first shelter for the purpose of religious services. John Smith recorded this beginning in his *Advertisements for the Unexperienced Planters of New England:*

When we first went to Virginia, I well remember, we did hang an awning (which is an old saile) to three or four trees to shadow us from the Sunne, our walles were rales of wood, our seats unhewed trees, till we cut plankes; our Pulpit a bar of wood nailed to two neighboring trees; in foul weather we shifted into an old rotten tent, for we had few better, and this came by the way of adventure for new. This was our Church, till we built a homely thing like a barne.

Thus in 1607, four years before the completion of the King James Bible, the Church of England was established on the shores of the Atlantic. Thirteen years later, the Puritans would build their "city upon a hill." Thus, the foundation of this country was begun, and its first churches begun also.

Left: Rosette Window in the Cathedral of St. John the Divine in New York City.

The Bettmann Archive, Philip Gendreau

Great window in chancel of Old Brick Church.

Old Brick Church
Isle of Wight, Virginia

Twelve years after the settling of Jamestown, Sir Christopher Lawn settled on the James River and named his plantation the Isle of Wight. In February of 1631, an Act of Assembly was passed which states "in all such places where churches are wanting or decayed, the inhabitants are tyed to contribute towards the building of a church." The Old Brick on the Isle of Wight bears the date 1632 and probably exists because of the Act of 1631. This makes it the oldest church left standing in the original colonies.

The Old Brick probably took about twenty-five years to complete; the third story of the tower was added after 1650. The brick structure is Gothic in architecture and reminiscent of sixteenth-century England. Only three of these buttressed brick churches were built in Colonial America, and this is the only one still standing.

The church was certainly soundly built to remain over three hundred years. The original roof of cypress shingles, however, lasted only a century before it had to be replaced. During the Revolution, Colonel Tarleton's British troops camped around the church, but it escaped damage. In 1887, a storm destroyed a part of the roof and the east gable, but the weather damaged less than time and disuse.

Old Brick was allowed to remain unused for many years, but between 1887 and 1893 a restoration took place. About all that was done then was to replace the original diamond-shaped panes of clear glass in the great window in the chancel, with stained glass panes from Munich. The side windows are Tiffany glass.

By 1953, the foundations, roof, and walls were about to collapse, and finally some action was taken to preserve this landmark. Old Brick Church was declared a National Shrine. Restoration was again begun and continues. With the replacement of the great window in the chancel with clear diamond panes, restoration would be total, for Protestant churches of colonial days never used stained glass.

9

Bruton Parish Church
Williamsburg, Virginia

Bruton Parish Church is part of a restoration project which includes the whole city of Williamsburg. This grand project has been undertaken by John D. Rockefeller, Jr.

During Colonial days, Bruton Parish Church was the Court Church and the Chapel Royal of Virginia. The royal governor's pew is still marked. Bruton Parish was Anglican and the first church was built as early as 1647 for the English planters and their families who came to the new land. The church's history is replete with names of Americans known to every schoolchild. The first rector was a Rowland Jones, great-grandfather of Martha Washington. The parish probably got its name from the birthplace of an honored member. The inscription on the tomb of Sir Thomas Ludwell, just inside one entrance gives his birthplace "at Bruton, in the county of Sommerset, in the Kingdom of England."

In 1699 the colonial government moved its center from the older Jamestown to Williamsburg, and Bruton Parish Church became the official Anglican Church of Virginia. By then a second church had been built. Here is where all of the government officials met and took communion. No wonder that this second church became too small for the burgeoning congregation and, in 1711, the present structure was begun.

Bruton Church is the largest cruciform church in Virginia; but more importantly, it stands as a silent witness to events which shaped a young country. The governor and members of the House of Burgesses were seated in the transept. The west gallery was assigned to the students of the College of William and Mary; and its railing still bears the initials carved by those students two hundred years ago. The baptismal font is believed to have been brought from Jamestown in 1758 when that church was abandoned. Before this font George Washington stood as godfather for at least fourteen slaves baptized there. The wooden belfry houses the bell, aptly named the "Liberty Bell of Virginia." It defiantly peeled for the Declaration of Independence, Cornwallis's surrender, and the 1793 signing of the peace treaty with Great Britain.

Bruton Church was the parish of governors and patriots. Washington was vestryman for twelve years; and the list of members includes Thomas Jefferson, Patrick Henry, George Mason, and George Wythe. Within its walls and churchyard lie two royal governors, members of the governor's council, and presidents of William and Mary. In keeping with the spirit of democracy, beside these grand personages lie common soldiers of both the Continental and Confederate armies.

Old Ship Meeting House
Hingham, Massachusetts

Standing only a short distance from the spot of the Pilgrim's landing at Plymouth, Massachusetts, Old Ship Meeting House is the oldest frame house of worship in the United States, and one of the most unusual.

Old Ship is aptly named. The frame, which went up in three days in July of 1681, was made by ship's carpenters, and resembles the curved timber and knees of a ship. Adding to the ship's design, are the captain's walk in the turret, the compasses beneath the spire and the sounding board over the pulpit.

The first pastor of the church was Peter Hobart, a graduate of Oxford who came to America in 1635. His successor, John Norton, was a graduate of the new school the Puritans had built for the training of their ministers: Harvard. It was Norton who built the second meeting house which still stands.

Here, General Benjamin Lincoln, who received the sword of Cornwallis at Yorktown, attended services. Another Lincoln, Samuel, who was an ancestor of President Lincoln, came to America in 1637 and is buried in the Old Ship graveyard.

This church, so securely linked with the Pilgrim heritage, figured prominently in the later Unitarian movement. The third pastor of Old Ship, Dr. Ebenezer Gay, is called "The first American Unitarian." A story is told of Dr. Gay: He and a friend were riding to Boston; they passed the gallows by Roxbury Neck. His companion teasingly asked, "Where would you be, my friend, if those gallows had their due?" Gay's reply was, "Riding alone to Boston."

In 1920 the Old Ship was restored to its original condition. A false ceiling which had been built below the beams and trusses in 1731 was torn out, exposing the beauty of the 150-year-old curved supports. The original pulpit, dating from 1755, was located and thirty-two of the eighty pew doors found and restored. Most of these doors were owned by the descendants of the original pew owners; and many are still marked with the names of those members.

Standing so close to that historic spot where the *Mayflower* discharged her passengers, Old Ship stands as a reminder of those small yet sturdy craft which brought men of vision and strong faith to a wilderness they were determined to tame.

St. Michael's Church

Charleston, South Carolina

In 1663, Charles II of England granted the charter of Carolina to eight noblemen; and in 1670 a settlement, Charles Towne, was established at the confluence of the Ashley and Cooper Rivers. One of the Lords Proprietors, Anthony Ashley Cooper, had as his secretary the philosopher John Locke who devised a "fundamental Constitution" for governing the province. The constitution provided religious freedom for the colony of South Carolina from its beginning. The king's religion was to be followed in Carolina, but freedom of worship was granted to every church or profession as long as its members believed in God and His public worship. This religious freedom in Carolina was equalled only by Rhode Island.

St. Michael's was the second church built in Charleston, South Carolina, and its building committee included the elite of the province. It stands today as the foremost example of Georgian architecture, with its stuccoed and painted brick, gleaming white in the Southern sun. The architect's name has long been lost, but the building's design is believed to be one of James Gibbs's from his *A Book of Architecture* (London: 1720). It was common practice to use designs from this book.

St. Michael's took eleven years to complete. Lack of funds, a hurricane that flooded the lower floor and spoiled much of the materials, and the French and Indian War all slowed down or halted construction. The scrolled iron gates of the church are among the most beautiful in a city known for ornamental ironwork. The interior furnishings are of cypress and cedar. The chancel has a gilded wrought-iron railing purchased in England in 1772; and the pulpit is richly carved. A great forty-two light chandelier was imported from England in 1803 and hangs over the pews. Materials for the construction and decoration, including slate, glass and iron, were imported from England and Holland.

All the brick was fired at Parnassus Plantation on Back River. That included both the common and molded brick, the curved brick for the Tuscan columns of the portico, and special brick for the cornice and molding.

continued

Courtesy Charleston Trident Chamber of Commerce

Interior of St. Michael's Church

St. Michael's bells have had a unique history. The first vestry meeting in 1762 planned for a set of eight bells. These were ordered in 1763 from Lester and Peck, a firm in England which also cast the Liberty Bell. The bells of St. Michael's rang out for the first time on July 21, 1764; and for the next eighteen years they sounded the alarms for fire and battle, struck the time, peeled in mourning, and summoned congregations to worship.

Then, in 1782, British officers claimed them as spoils of war and shipped them back to England. There, they were bought by the successors to Lester and Peck, the firm of Chapman and Mears. After years of appeals, St. Michael's won the bells back, so they recrossed the ocean and were gratefully hung by the parishioners in Charleston.

During the years of the Civil War, the great bell, called "Great Michael" was retained in the belfry to sound alarms. The other bells were taken to Columbia and stored in a shed at the State House for safekeeping.

When Sherman burned Columbia on February 17, 1865, the State House and its adjoining shed were ruined. After the war, five of the bells were recovered; two had just disappeared. The five were shipped back to Charleston to join Great Michael which had since cracked. In 1867, all six were sent back to England, again to the firm of Mears and Stainbank, the successor to Chapman. They were recast, returned to Charleston, and rehung in the steeple of St. Michael's after their fifth crossing of the Atlantic.

Today, the steeple of St. Michael's remains illuminated at night as a landmark for ships at sea and as a symbol to those on shore of America's determination to freely worship God.

Illuminated steeple of
St. Michael's Church

Courtesy Massachusetts Department of Commerce and Development Division of Tourism

King's Chapel
Boston, Massachusetts

In contrast to the freedom which existed in South Carolina, this first Episcopal Church in New England was born out of hostility. The Puritans left England as dissenters from the Church of England and had established three Congregational churches in Boston. When the English of the colony needed a place to worship, the Anglican governor, Edmund Andros, forced them to share the Old South Meeting House. The Puritans had to wait for their meetings until the Anglican service was over. The result was two years of joint use of the Old South, but under great hostility until the governor again intervened. He ordered a corner of burying ground be set aside for a church. Building began in 1688.

By 1741, however, the congregation needed a larger building. In 1744 work was begun on the present King's Chapel, designed by Peter Harrison. Although the original design called for a spire, the money ran out and it was never built. There remains only a tower.

The bell which hangs in the tower of King's Chapel is probably the most famous of Paul Revere's bells. It is also the largest, weighing over a ton. This great bell once tolled the deaths of the community—three times three strokes for a man, three times two for a woman, plus a stroke for each year of life.

The exterior of King's Chapel is gray granite, but the interior is opulent. Its elaborate three-decker pulpit, constructed in 1717, is the oldest in the United States. The altar is carved and gilded; embodied in it are four painted canvas panels which were drawn in England and brought over in July 1696, along with the altar table beneath. The organ case dates back to 1756 and is ornately carved. According to tradition, the organ was selected by Friedrich Handel.

While Massachusetts was under British rule, King's Chapel served as the Chapel Royal. The splendor of the interior did not escape notice of the Puritans in Boston and intensified the hostility between the British Anglicans and the Puritans. After the British were driven from Boston in 1776, the congregation of Old South worshiped at King's Chapel until their own church was repaired. This sharing did much to heal the wound the forced sharing of Old South had caused.

This first Episcopal Church in New England which was such a thorn to the Puritans, became a dissenter itself. It later became the first Unitarian church in America.

St. George's Church
Philadelphia, Pennsylvania

The first group of Methodists in the United States was small and met for a time in a sail loft on Dock Street. During 1767, Thomas Webb, the leader of the Society, named the group St. George's Society in honor of the patron saint of England. The membership grew and meetings moved to a former public house. By 1769 the Society had one hundred members.

The Methodists wished to build a chapel but had little money. They managed to buy the shell of a building begun by the German Reformed Church for seven hundred pounds. This price, however, didn't include the ground the church stood on; this they rented until 1802.

St. George's had a dirt floor until after the Revolution. The first three Conferences of American Methodism, the first held in 1773, was held on the dirt floor of the unplastered, unpainted building. By 1790, the floor was completed; and benches more comfortable than the slat-backed original ones were installed. But not until 1784 were the walls plastered.

The people of Philadelphia are protecting this bit of history. The route of the Benjamin Franklin bridge over the Delaware River had originally been planned directly over the church. It was moved fourteen feet, however, in order to save the building. Now a high retaining wall stands in front of St. George's Church which is a part of Independence National Historical Park.

The Saal
Ephrata, Pennsylvania

Main room of The Saal

In 1735, the first Protestant monastery in America was founded. It was begun by the Society of the Solitary, a secessionist group of the Church of the Brethren (German Baptists). The first name of the community was *Kloster* (Cloister) but nicknamed "Dunkerstown," because the group was known as "Dunkards." In 1738, the organizer of the Society in America, Johann Konrad Beissel, renamed the Christian commune Ephrata, which was the ancient name of Bethlehem.

The community grew until the *Berghaus*, or community house, became too small. Another house, named the *Kedar*, was built in 1735. One room of this building was set aside for worship. The members lived in the smaller rooms, the men on the first level and the women on the second.

This building also became too small, so in 1741 the Saal was built. Originally only two stories, it became the house of worship for the whole community. The architecture was uniquely American, but the roof, typical of many built in Germany, has a very steep pitch and a number of dormer windows. The inner walls were filled with stone between the timbers and then plastered with clay mixed with straw, then again with white plaster. The wide-planked ceiling of the main room, plain tables and benches, and an unadorned wooden lectern give the room a warm and rustic look.

Music was an important part of the religious life at The Saal. Over two thousand pieces of music were copied by the sisters until the brethren installed a printing press.

Other industries of the community were spinning and weaving of linens and carpets, pottery making, and basket weaving.

The Society of the Solitary abided by a strict code which forbade fighting wars. The Cloister, however, opened its doors to the wounded and the dying soldiers of the Battle of Brandywine. A number of them are buried on Zion Hill at The Saal; and the community lost several buildings which had to be burned to prevent the spread of typhus.

After the Revolution, the community began to decline until, in 1934, the Society was formally dissolved. In 1941 the property was absorbed by the Pennsylvania Historical and Museum Commission which restored the buildings and opened them to the public.

Chapel is to the right

Old Trappe Church
Trappe, Pennsylvania

Old Trappe is the oldest Lutheran Church in the United States. It was built in 1743 by the founder of the Lutheran Church in America, Heinrich Melchior Muhlenberg. Muhlenberg was born in 1711 in Halle, Germany, and came to America in 1742 as a Pietist missionary. Pietists sought to revitalize Christian living by a return to the principles of Luther.

In 1730, Muhlenberg organized a congregation in Pennsylvania. For the next thirteen years, church services were held in a barn. Muhlenberg designed the new church, to be built of stone; construction began in 1743 and was completed by the fall of 1745. For more than a century, the Trappe congregation held services in the church. By 1852, however, a larger church was needed and one was built not far from the first.

The old stone church is preserved almost in its original condition. The stone floor, however, is covered by boards and the stone walls are stuccoed. The organ, imported from Europe, is still there, the organ so necessary for the Lutheran services which featured singing in harmony. The high-backed pews are also original ones. Some pews still bear the locks, used by the more prosperous members; other pews were left open. In these pews, as in most colonial churches, men and women worshiped separated by the center aisle.

Old Chapel
Bethlehem, Pennsylvania

Because of the day, and in memory of the Birth of our dear Saviour, we went into the stable in the tenth hour and sang with feeling, so that our hearts melted.

Nicht Jerusalem, Sondern Bethlehem, Aus dir Dommet, was mir Frommet.

(Not Jerusalem, But Bethlehem—From thee comes that which benefits me.)

and Moravia. Some settled in Germany on the estate of Count Ludwig von Zinzendorf who subsequently sponsored their settlements in America.

In this country, the Moravians first settled in Georgia, then came to Pennsylvania in 1740 as Georgia became involved in war with Florida. Rather than becoming embroiled in that conflict, they left their five-year settlement. Led by Peter Bohler, they came to Philadelphia, a haven from persecution. In 1741, they acquired five hundred acres of land at the juncture of Lehigh River and Monocacy Creek.

Throughout its history, the Bethlehem settlement gave music an important part in their lives and in their services. The year after its founding, the settlement held a *Singstunde*; and in 1744, they organized a *Collegium Musicum*. This event was continued each year, until in 1820 it became the Philharmonic Society, an instrumental and oratorio group. Another continuing tradition, began in 1754, is the Easter sunrise service accompanied by a trombone choir.

Moravians published several of Bach's works even before they were published in Europe. In 1882, the Bethlehem Choral Union was formed and grew into the Bethlehem Bach Festival. Even today, two days in May are set aside for the singing and playing of the music of Johann Sebastian Bach. Always included is the B Minor Mass. In 1905, the Bach Festival was held at the church; but since 1912, it has taken place across the river at Lehigh University.

The Moravian community of Bethlehem accomplished a great deal in mission work among the Indians. Relations with the Indians were so peaceful that during the French and Indian War, Bethlehem became the white settlers' refuge. The Indians supplied them with venison. The building which today stands at the center of the Moravian settlement, was the mission building in which many Indians were converted. This commitment to spreading the gospel to the Indians was the center of the faith.

Thus was the Moravian settlement at Bethlehem, Pennsylvania, established. The Old Chapel, completed in 1742, still stands. It was built between the Gemeinhaus and Bell House, using the walls of these buildings as its own.

The Moravian Church was begun by John Huss of Bohemia who died at the stake in 1457. The Moravians were then driven from Bohemia

Touro Synagogue
Newport, Rhode Island

Roger Williams founded the colony of Rhode Island in 1636 on the principle of liberty of conscience. The Code of Laws of 1647 concluded: "All men may walk as their consciences persuade them, everyone in the name of his God." It is somehow fitting that Touro is the only extant colonial synagogue in the United States.

The Jews who immigrated to the colonies were Sephardic, descendants of those who fled to Spain and Portugal after the capture of Jerusalem by Titus in 70 A.D. Most who came to the American colony were prosperous merchants from Holland; and they established their community in Newport, what was then the center of colonial trade.

By 1658, a few Jews arrived in Newport and in 1677 they purchased land for a burial ground. (It subsequently became the subject of Longfellow's poem "The Jewish Cemetery at Newport.") Worship services were held in private homes until 1759 when construction began on the present building. The designer was Peter Harrison of Newport. An importer by profession, architecture was only his hobby and he designed the synagogue without pay. He also designed King's Chapel in Boston and Christ Church, Cambridge, Massachusetts.

Touro was under construction for four years before it was completed. On the first day of Hanukkah, December 2, 5523 (1763), the synagogue was dedicated by the rabbi, Dr. Isaac de Abraham Touro. The Books of the Laws were deposited in the Georgian styled Ark. One of these books is a treasure of the synagogue, being about 400 years old. It was brought by the Sephardic Jews from Spain during the Inquisition.

Touro Synagogue is built in Spanish style and incorporates features from the mother synagogue in Amsterdam. The building remains unchanged on the outside as well as inside; the brick is still painted tan. One unusual feature is that the seats are not facing the Ark, but are at right angles to it. The men use the ground floor, and the galleries for women are supported on three sides by twelve columns of superimposed Corinthian over Ionic which represent the twelve tribes of Israel.

In 1790, President Washington visited Newport on a tour to inspire the citizens to their new responsibilities. He was addressed on behalf of the Hebrew congregation by Moses Seixas who said:

Deprived as we heretofore have been of the invaluable rights of free citizens, we now (with a deep sense of gratitude to the Almighty Dispenser of all Events) behold a Government erected by the amnesty of the people, a Government which gives to bigotry no sanction, to persecution no assistance; but generously affording to all liberty of conscience and immunities of citizenship, deeming everyone, of whatever nation, tongue, or language, equal parts of the great Governmental machine.

The Revolution and British occupation of Newport dispersed the Jewish community. The synagogue closed. Not until 1883 could the synagogue be reopened. In 1947, the Touro Synagogue was rededicated as a National Historic site by the National Park Service.

26

First Baptist
Providence, Rhode Island

In 1636, Roger Williams was tried by the Puritan officials at Boston, found guilty, and banished from the colony of Massachusetts. Williams had opposed church authorities on several points. These included, among others, that civil authorities had no jurisdiction over men's consciences. Williams also believed that since the Indians were the true owners of the land, the King had no right to grant charters. At one time, he even proposed cutting the cross out of the British Union Jack.

To avoid deportation to England, Williams and his small band of dissenters fled to the south. There, Pilgrims controlled the land. These Pilgrims in Plymouth differed from the Puritans to the north. They offered the small band sanctuary in their territory. When Williams arrived in safety, he named the place Providence out of gratitude to God's mercy.

Two years after the settlement at Providence, Williams and eleven other men formed the first Baptist church in America; Williams becoming the church's first pastor. After a few months, however, he withdrew to continue his role as a "seeker." Roger Williams was the first man to proclaim true religious liberty in America; and Rhode Island was the first colony to identify with the principle of religious freedom.

For the first sixty years, the congregation met in private homes or outdoors. The present meeting house was begun in 1774 and dedicated in May 1775. In keeping with the founder's spirit of individual worth, the design for the church was drawn by Joseph Brown who was an amateur architect and student of math, astronomy and philosophy. Brown used as his guide *The Book of Architecture, Designs, and Ornaments* (London: 1728) by James Gibbs who was a pupil of Sir Christopher Wren.

First Baptist serves a dual purpose. Rhode Island College (now Brown University) was founded in 1764; but in 1771 it was moved to Providence. The prospectus for the new meeting house stated that the building be "for Publick Worship of Almighty God, and also for holding Commencement in." For almost 200 years, it has served in both capacities.

The exterior of the church is original, except for the spire which has been renewed. Inside, little has been changed. In 1834, the original gallery for slaves, freedmen, and Indians was removed; otherwise, the interior is preserved. One addition has been the stained glass window, donated in 1884. Focal point of the interior is the gleaming crystal chandelier brought from England in 1792. It was presented to the church as a gift from Hope Brown in memory of her father. It was first lighted for her marriage; once lit by candles, it now glows by electricity.

The bell hanging in the steeple of the First Baptist peels every sunrise, noon, and evening at nine P.M. Cast in London, the engraved inscription on the bell reads:

For freedom of conscience the town was first
*   planted,*
Persuasion, not force, was used by the people;
This church is the oldest, and has not recanted,
Enjoying and granting bell, temple and steeple.

Only in the colonies could a nonconformist house of worship be called a church and have both steeple and bell.

"Congress shall make no law respecting an establishment of religion, or prohibiting the free exercise thereof . . ."

Constitution of the United States

Bulwarks of Patriotism

The houses of God have served not only as places of worship and praise to God, but at times have been subjected to occupation by enemy forces as well as gatherings of the defenders.

The church of St. John at Richmond, Virginia, is one of these historic places. Built in 1741, it was host to the Second Virginia Convention in 1775. Washington was there and Thomas Jefferson, too. But to the left of the aisle and toward the front of the church a man stood up that day in St. John's and shouted what became the rallying cry for the next few years. The man was Patrick Henry, and he ended his speech with the now familiar words, "Give me Liberty, or give me Death!"

Other patriots came to St. John's. In the churchyard lies George Wythe, the first signer of the Declaration of Independence. Because of Wythe and Henry, St. John's has often been called the "Birthplace of Liberty." Many other churches, also, stand as monuments to the opening struggle of American history.

St. John's Church in
Richmond, Virginia

Freelance Photographers Guild

St. Peter's Church
New Kent County, Virginia

St. Peter's was the site of the marriage of George and Martha Washington, on January 6, 1759. A traditional account of the ceremony makes it sound like a very festive occasion.

Washington and Mrs. Custis rode to the Church in a chariot and the invited persons followed them in vehicles of various shapes. When they stood up before the minister to be married, Washington towered beside his betrothed, who looked unusually small and low in stature. Washington was in uniform, and Mrs. Custis was arrayed in a fine white silk dress. All the servants on the White House estate were given a holiday, and all in holiday attire joined in the general merry-making that followed.

(The White House in this account was not the presidential home in Washington, D.C. but the home of Martha Custis.)

St. Peter's is a plain, low-pitched building. It was constructed at a cost of 164,000 pounds of tobacco. This was not an unusual method of payment for the time and the locale, but rather, the accepted currency. The steeple of St. Peter's wasn't built until twelve years after the bulk of the church.

This old English, brick church sits deep in the woods about thirty miles west of Williamsburg and twenty miles east of Richmond, Virginia. In 1922, St. Peter's Church Restoration Association began to take the necessary steps to save this historic building. Today, it is largely restored and is a tribute to America's first presidential family; the church known as "The first church of the first First Lady."

Old South was born of strife in 1662 when twenty-nine members of the First Church of Boston seceded from that church in opposition to the requirement of church membership for citizenship in the colony. The first building of the church was a two-story edifice of cedar, built in 1699. This was the last residence of John Winthrop, the first governor of Massachusetts and the church in which Benjamin Franklin was baptized. This first church building also saw Judge Samuel Sewell, who had presided at the Salem witchcraft trials publicly confess his errors, after some forceful encouragement from Old South pastor, Samuel Willard.

Strife returned to Old South when Sir Edmund Andros came to Boston to assume the post of Royal Governor of the colony. He demanded that one of the two Puritan churches be turned over for Church of England services. As a result, each Sunday for the next two years, the Old South congregation remained outside until Anglican services were concluded.

This sharing of the meeting house, however, caused a breech between the Puritans and Anglicans not to be quickly healed. During the occupation of Boston by the British, General Burgoyne ripped out all the church pews save one. That pew served as a pigstye and the sanctuary became a riding ring for the Queen's Light Dragoons.

Only three months after the governor's arrival, his wife died. The funeral of Lady Andros was held at night in a candlelit Old South. Soldiers lined the funeral route from the governor's mansion to the church as the hearse drawn by six horses made its way down the torchlit route to the Anglican King's Chapel Burying Ground.

In 1729, building began on the second and present building, the one which served as a stable for the British. Prior to the Revolution, this building was the site of many rallys and meetings. Probably the most famous began on December 4, 1773, when seven thousand people gathered around Old South in opposition to the British tax on tea imports. The crowd listened to the rhetoric of Sam Adams and Josiah Quincy. Around six in the evening, word spread through the crowd that Governor Hutchinson would not allow the British ships to leave the harbor without first unloading the cargo of tea. Immediately upon hearing this news, Samuel Adams leaped to his feet and shouted, "This meeting can do nothing more to save the country." The crowd then dispersed. Some dressed as Indians and made their way to the harbor and threw the ship's cargo into the water. The Boston Tea Party, and perhaps the Revolution, began at Old South.

In 1876, however, the Old South Meeting house was auctioned off as junk. The women of Massachusetts purchased the building, the site of so much history, and now preserve it as a historical landmark.

Old South Meeting House
Boston, Massachusetts

Courtesy Massachusetts Department of Commerce and Development, Division of Tourism

A. Devaney, Inc.

Old North Church
Boston, Massachusetts

Old North Church has been standing on Copp's Hill since 1723 when it was built mainly by donations from the congregation of King's Chapel, its mother church. This is the oldest church still standing in Boston and probably the most famous steeple in the country.

This steeple of Paul Revere fame was first raised in 1740 to a height of 195 feet. It blew down in 1804 and was rebuilt twenty feet lower. A peal of eight bells was hung in 1744, one bearing the inscription, "The first ring cast for the British empire in North America, 1744." Bell number four bears the words, "God preserve the Church of England." Paul Revere, as a boy, rang those bells, so was quite familiar with the steeple which held lanterns, according to Longfellow's poem "One if by land, two if by sea." A statue of Paul Revere on horseback stands in the park behind the church.

This steeple was the site in 1757 of the first flight by an American. A Mr. John Childs flew off this steeple while connected to it by a rope. He performed this, according to a newsletter of the day, before "a great number of spectators." The event caused such a clamor that Childs repeated his act, but this time he buckled on two loaded pistols to his belt, planning to fire them on the way down. The guns misfired, however, so he had to recock them and fire them on his flight back up the steeple. The more circumspect Bostonians, however, put a stop to this circus-like performance on the steeple of their revered house of worship.

Old North contains other treasures in addition to its steeple. At the front of the church stand four carved wooden figures presented in 1746 by the captain of the privateer, *Queen of Hungary*. The figures were on their way to grace a convent on the St. Lawrence River. The lovely old chandeliers were also bounty gotten from another French vessel during the French and Indian War of 1746.

In 1912, the church was restored to its colonial condition, and pews were marked with the names of the original holders. In 1954 the steeple was again blown down, this time by a hurricane. Donations flowed in from all over the country for its restoration—for, indeed, all Americans hold dear the steeple of Boston's Old North Church.

Courtesy Old North Church

Courtesy Old North Church

Opposite left: Statue of Paul Revere behind Old North. Opposite lower right: Pulpit of Old North. Above: View of the Sanctuary showing altar, great window and one of the chandeliers presented by Captain William Maxwell. The candles are still lit for afternoon and evening services. Right: Organ built in 1759 by Thomas Johnston of Boston and Avery-Bennett clock, built in 1726.

Courtesy Old North Church

View of the chancel and altar before
the Palladian window and great organ.

Sanctuary with wineglass pulpit and box pews.

St. Peter's Church
Philadelphia, Pennsylvania

In Philadelphia they built St. Peter's on land donated by the sons of William Penn. Services have been held since 1761. The interior remains original, and exquisite with the rare wineglass pulpit at one end of the center aisle and the chancel and altar at the other end before the Palladian window. The box pews line the length of the building, so worshipers must either shift from one side of the aisle to the opposite pew or sit with their backs to part of the service.

The tower and steeple with chimes were added in 1842. Many bells of colonial churches have their own history and those of St. Peter's are no exception. Before the British occupied the city in 1777, the two bells of St. Peter's, along with those of Christ Church and the Liberty Bell, were carried through the lines. They were hidden beneath the floor of the Zion Reformed Church in Allentown until the end of the British occupation.

The Revolution caused other changes at St. Peter's. In 1777, Jacob Duché became rector of both St. Peter's and Christ Church. On July 4, 1776, he called a special meeting of the vestry. They voted to omit prayers for the King at both churches and Duché was appointed the first Congressional chaplain. Three months later, however, Duché resigned. He had thought the Declaration only a bluff. He wrote General Washington, urging him to desert. Feeling against Duché was so high that he sailed for England in 1777. After the Constitution was adopted, and with President Washington's pardon, Duché returned to Philadelphia. He is buried in the churchyard of St. Peter's.

Left: Chancel of Christ Church. The Palladian window was the first of this design in America. Opposite: The two-hundred-foot steeple is called "The Philadelphia Steeple." The Royal Crown of England which first surmounted the steeple was destroyed by lightning in 1779. A bishop's mitre is now at the top.

Christ Church
Philadelphia, Pennsylvania

Longfellow used the sonorous bells of Christ Church to set the scene in the closing portion of *Evangeline:*

Distant and soft on her ear fell the chimes from the belfry of Christ Church,
While, intermingled with these, across the meadows were wafted
Sounds of psalms, that were sung by the Swedes in the church at Wicaco.

These bells are still treasured by Christ Church. The first bell dates from 1702 although the peal of eight bells was not brought from London until 1754. Benjamin Franklin helped raise the money for their purchase by managing the "Philadelphia Steeple Lottery."

The history of Christ Church is that of the "first" Anglican church in the colony, physically and socially. Christ Church was founded in 1695 by thirty-six men, including a judge of the Admiralty, an Attorney General, numerous physicians, lawyers and two men which legend, or tradition, calls pirates. Its list of past members include such famous names as George Washington, John Penn, John Adams, and Benjamin Franklin. The list of worshipers extends farther and includes the entire Continental Congress which attended as a group on July 20, 1775, the General Convention which met here in 1785, and over 20,000 mourners at the funeral of Benjamin Franklin.

The present church was begun in 1727 as an enlargement of the second church. The first Christ Church had been built of logs in 1695 and was long since gone. Through the years, changes have occurred in the present church. In 1834, the high-backed pews were replaced with lower, more modern ones and one pew, that belonging to George and Martha Washington, was sent to the National Museum in Washington, D. C. The church retains communion silver which was a gift of Queen Anne, presented in 1708.

Christ Church is such a part of America's history that in 1952, it was designated a national shrine by an Act of Congress.

"In France I had almost always seen the spirit of religion and the spirit of freedom pursuing courses diametrically opposed to each other; but in America I found that they were intimately united, and that they reigned in common over the same country."

Alexis de Tocqueville

Missions Across the Land

Missions began in this country when the Spanish arrived with their religious leaders whose aim was the conversion of the native. These missions, for the most part, were not meant to be permanent; and few remain today. A second type of mission, however, sprang up along the expanding frontier as Americans and immigrants began their westward trek. These churches were aided by home churches, either in Europe or in the eastern part of this country.

One such frontier church was St. Paul's Episcopal Church in Tombstone, Arizona. Here, in the wildest mining camp in the west, the citizens built a church of adobe brick, hauling by oxen the necessary timber from the mountains. The result was a source of civic pride and became a symbol of civilization in an uncivilized town. The church even seemed to calm the town down a bit. Local pride liked to exclaim: "Bloody Tombstone could plant a rosebush and build a church."

These frontier missions generally became permanent houses of worship. Today, many have grown into great and newer buildings with large congregations. Many, too, later sponsored missions of their own in response to the ongoing push of civilization.

Little Brown Church in the Vale
Nashua, Iowa

There really is a "church in the wildwood, a little brown church in the vale." The church about which the song was written was built during the Civil War for the congregation of the First Congregational Church, formed in 1855. Land, lumber and material were contributed by the members who also donated their labors for the construction. The bell in the tower was given by a couple in New York and was such a wonder to the members that it rang constantly during its trip from Dubuque to Nashua.

The hymn "Little Brown Church in the Vale" was written by the Rev. William S. Pitts in 1857. Pitts was traveling by stagecoach through Nashua; and during a noon stopover, he walked up the streets to a wooded spot. No church was there in 1857, but Pitts wrote a song about one. When he returned to the spot after 1864 the church he envisioned stood on the spot.

The church opens its door each year to hundreds of couples who wish to be married in the "little brown church in the vale."

Courtesy Iowa Development Commission

Old Fort
Niagara, New York

In the French Castle of Old Fort Niagara, there is a Jesuit Chapel which has served three nationalities, and two religions. The Fort is at the northwest tip of New York state on the border of the vast territory, extending from Quebec to Louisiana, explored and claimed by the French.

The first Fort was a crude wooden house surrounded by a palisade, built in 1679 by René Robert Cavelier de La Salle, the explorer who tried to extend the French empire through North America. La Salle moved up the St. Lawrence River to this point at the mouth of the Niagara River and founded Fort Conty, one of sixty forts built by the French.

That fort burned and another was built in 1687. This one was named Fort Denonville. This fort was built as a defense against the Iroquois and the English; but during peacetime it served as a trading post. The French had to obtain permission from the Iroquois to build a "House of Peace." The Indians were not told, of course, that the entire third floor was to be a gun deck and the dormer windows to be gun ports. A room on the second floor was set aside as a Jesuit chapel, one of the first Christian churches on this frontier.

In 1762, the present stone building was begun and named Fort Niagara. After the long siege in 1759, Fort Niagara fell to the British. When they took over, they built an Anglican chapel in front near the present flagpoles; but they stripped the French chapel of its furnishings. The English held the fort until the Treaty of Ghent in 1815. This treaty gave the property to the United States. Thus, the fort has flown the flags of three different nations in succession. Today, all three flags fly together: French, English, and American.

From 1927 to 1934 the chapel underwent a thorough restoration according to plans found in the Colonial Archives of the French War Department. All furnishings are handcarved reproductions of the originals, and the restored chapel has been consecrated as a place of worship. The fort and castle are now open to the public under the administration of the Old Fort Niagara Association.

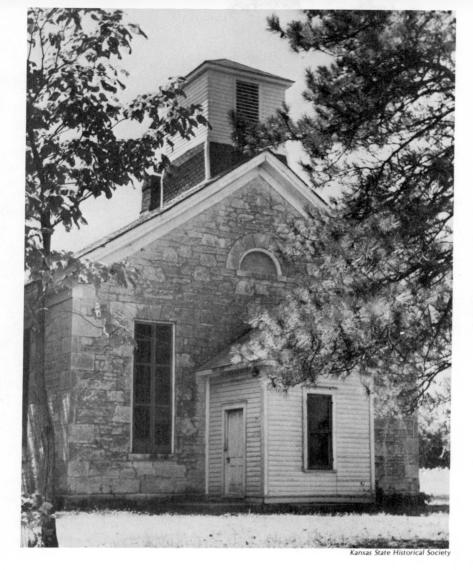
Kansas State Historical Society

Beecher Bible and Rifle Church
Wabaunsee, Kansas

In the mid-nineteenth century, a colony of Puritans moved from New Haven, Connecticut, to Kansas. They were on a mission to establish a Congregational church in the west and to promote the settlement of Kansas by an anti-slavery element. Back in Connecticut, one hundred prospective members had raised enough money for the trip and additional funds to get by until the first crop harvest. They didn't, however, have enough money for weapons needed for the protection against wild animals and Indians.

The Reverend Henry Ward Beecher, pastor of Plymouth Church in Brooklyn, New York, heard of the project. He was so enthusiastic that he vowed to obtain whatever additional money was necessary for the project. One week after he returned to Brooklyn, he had enough money to send each member to Kansas with $625, a Bible, and a hymnbook. The money was to buy a Sharpe's rifle or Carbine, then the most effective small arm.

The group settled in Kansas and founded the Beecher Bible and Rifle Church in 1856. Services were at first in a grove of trees, later in a tent, then in a temporary church. The present stone church was built in 1862. In the tradition of old, the actual building was done by the congregation. The sanctuary is built in native stone quarried in the nearby Blue Stem hills and hauled to the site. Woodwork was native wood, sawed in the saw-mill that had been brought from New England.

During the "Bleeding Kansas" era, rifles were shipped free to state settlers in boxes labeled "Bibles." Pro-slavery advocates in Missouri passed by them when they searched wagons and steamboats hauling freight to the new settlers. The Sharp rifles came to be known as "Beecher Bibles."

The Beecher Bible and Rifle church stands as a symbol of the American westward movement, when settlers came to a new frontier with a Bible under one arm and a rifle under the other.

Mural depicting the historical and religious
life of the community of St. Augustine.

Cathedral of St. Augustine
St. Augustine, Florida

The Cathedral of St. Augustine overlooks
the Plaza de la Constitución and is often
called the "Birthplace of a Nation."

The Spaniards came to the New World in
search of gold and the secret of youth. Ponce de
León landed at what is now St. Augustine, search-
ing for the legendary Fountain of Youth, in 1513.
After him, in 1765, Pedro Menéndez de Avilés
came to crush a Huguenot settlement; he stayed
and founded St. Augustine in 1765.

With the Spaniards, came their religious
faith. In 1565, Francisco López de Mendoze
Grajales, a Spanish missionary founded the
country's first mission, Nombre de Dios. Florida,
however, was never a vital part of New Spain, so
it wasn't until 1784 that the King of Spain sent
two Irish priests to Florida to build both a school
and a church. The Reverend Thomas Hassett
founded America's first free school, and Father
Michael O'Reilly built the Cathedral of St.
Augustine.

Of Spanish design, work on school and
church was begun in 1791. Some of the building
material came from the shrines of Tolemato, an
Indian mission and Nuestra Señora de la Leche, a
Spanish mission which had been destroyed by the
British. Additional Coquina rock for the building
was quarried from Anastasia Island which lies
across the river from the city. The stone had to be
cut by hand and ferried by barge to the building site.

The design of the church is Spanish with a
Moroccan belfry. The cathedral boasts twelve
stained glass windows which relate the conversion of Saint Augustine from paganism to
Christianity.

The cathedral partially burned in 1887. Some
believe that the heat from the blaze fused the soft
coquina rock walls into their present granite-like
hardness. The fire destroyed the belfry, however,
so a campanile was erected with a chime of bells
and a clock.

A sundial which was originally on the church
facade is now lodged below the clock. The Latin
inscription on the dial reads: "The hours perish
and we must account for them." The Cathedral of
St. Augustine accounts for 200 years.

Courtesy St. Augustine and St. Johns
County Chamber of Commerce

43

Spanish Missions

The mission was a vital institution to the spread of the Spanish Empire during the fifteenth and seventeenth centuries. Although the padres set forth to spread Christianity, the government sponsored the missions for political reasons.

There were three ways Spain extended her empire: by the *presidio* (fort), *pueblo* (town), and by the mission. Of the three, the mission was the most inexpensive, served as a nucleus for the future town, and became self-supporting. These missions were designed to be only temporary frontier establishments. In most cases, they remain today only as monuments to their past work.

The mission was to civilize and educate the Indian. The original task was to teach him to read and write in his own language. There were so many dialects of Indian, however, that the padres taught Spanish, the language which still thrives in the Southwest, the area of Spanish Missions.

The missions were all built on a similar plan. The core of the mission was typically a large and rambling four-sided building, built around a square courtyard. Around the inner side of this building was an arcade connecting workshops, living quarters, and dining rooms. This square building served as a wall and had only one or two doors which were blocked at night.

Central to the enclosure was the church, the largest and most imposing building of the mission. The church was always built of the best available materials and decorated with the loveliest and most ornate furnishings the people could secure. Rising above the building was a campanile containing bells usually brought from Mexico City or even Peru. The bells summoned the Indians to work and to pray.

Ed Cooper

Left: Statue of Father Serra, who established nine of the twenty-one California missions, stands in the courtyard of the mission at San Juan Capistrano. Above: View of San Xavier del Bac Mission from the inside.

45

San Juan Mission
Capistrano, California

The Mission of San Juan Capistrano began in 1775 when Father Lasuén set up a cross and dedicated the land to God. Eight days later, news of an Indian attack at San Diego Mission reached Capistrano. Father Lasuén buried the mission bells then took his party to the presidio at San Diego.

It was almost a year later, after peace had come to the territory, that the mission was reopened. This time, Father Serra went to Capistrano, dug up the bells, and hung them from a tree. After another year, the first small church of adobe was built.

The mission prospered and grew until by 1796 a larger church was built. Indians did most of the work, carrying stone from the quarry six miles away, dragging the small blocks by chain, the larger ones in carts and the smallest ones were carried by women and children. It took nine years to construct the mission church and when it was finished, in 1806, a two-day festival celebrated its completion. It stood as the most magnificent church of all the California missions—180 feet long and forty feet wide, the vaulted ceiling was surmounted by seven domes. The bell tower was visible for ten miles, the four bells heard all over the countryside.

The glorious mission church stood for only six years. In December of 1812 as the bells began to ring for the second mass, an earthquake hit the

Alpha Photo Associates

area. The vault of the church split open, the walls swayed, and the massive stone ceiling buried forty of the kneeling congregation. The bells fell from the tower. The original adobe church was not damaged.

The following year the bells were rehung in one of the walls, and the little adobe church was used once more.

The mission of Capistrano is the subject of many legends. Because the bells are hung by ropes attached to their clappers, they can ring by themselves in the wind. This gives rise to tales of their pealing in response to romance and tragedy. The most famous legend of Capistrano, of course, is that of the return of the swallows. They arrive each spring on St. Joseph's Day.

Carmel Mission
Carmel-by-the-Sea, California

Of the California missions, the church at Carmel is probably the most beautiful with its Moorish looking towers and rough sandstone exterior against a background of the sea. It was begun by Father Junipero Serra who established nine of the twenty-one California missions. The Carmel mission was founded in 1770 at the presidio of Monterey. Dedication ceremonies took place amid the firing of muskets and roaring of cannons which frightened the Indians so much that they went into hiding. Serra soon found, however, that the land at Monterey would not support a mission; so he moved the mission to a better site at Carmel valley.

In 1781, Serra ordered the stone quarried for a new church. He died only three years later. It was sixteen years before the church he envisioned was finished.

When the California missions were secularized, the land was sold right up to the walls of the church. It was necessary to later buy back a strip of land so that the church could be entered. The church at Carmel was left to rot, and the beams of the roof fell in. It stood without a roof for thirty years. The sand drifted in the broken doors and windows; and even grass and weeds grew profusely inside. A visitor to the church in 1861 wrote: "hundreds of squirrels scampered around their holes in the old walls; cattle had free access to all parts; and thousands of birds, apparently, lived in nooks in the old deserted walls."

Finally, a campaign was begun to repair the church for the centennial of Father Serra's death. About all that was done, however, was to replace the roof with one of shingles which was not in keeping with the mission architecture. It has since been replaced.

In the 1930s, restoration of the mission was undertaken in earnest. Today, the church has been restored to its original manner as much as possible. It has been classified as a basilica because of its historic importance and connection with Father Serra.

The church at Carmel, like its sister mission at Capistrano, provides a home to the cliff swallows which return each spring. They attach their nests to the stone next to the great Angelus bell; the ringing scatters them wildly.

The Alamo
San Antonio, Texas

The monks who came with the Spanish founded the Mission San Antonia de Valero in 1718 to minister to the Indians' needs. This mission, however, was ill-fated from the very beginning. The first building was destroyed by a hurricane. A second built nearby fell victim to a variety of disasters, not the least of which was smallpox.

By the early 1800s, Americans, lured by the prospect of open land, moved into the Southwest by the droves. In fact, so many Americans came to the area that the Mexican president closed the borders to immigrants, cutting off those already there.

Because of this isolation, Texas, in 1835, seceded from Mexico. The Mission San Antonio de Valero then became a fort in which the Americans gathered, only to be annihilated by the Mexicans. The Mission, known now only as the Alamo, remained a patriotic symbol; and *Remember the Alamo!* became the rallying cry for the subsequent Mexican-American War and ushered in Texas independence.

Today, the Alamo stands not as a house of worship, but as a testimony to freedom.

Nave of San Xavier del Bac.

San Xavier del Bac
Tucson, Arizona

During the seventeenth and eighteenth centuries, five missions for the Indians were built in Arizona. One remains. Beautiful and gleaming white in the desert sun, it is named San Xavier del Bac but called by the Indians, *La Paloma Blanca del Desierto*, "White Dove of the Desert."

San Xavier stands nine miles south of Tucson and takes its Spanish name from an early Indian settlement. The place was named *Bac*, the place where the waters appear, because of the Santa Cruz River which runs underground for some distance and then reappears near the settlement. The Sobaipuri Indians first lived in the area, later the Papagos Indians came from the western desert lands. The first missionary to the natives in this area was a Jesuit explorer, Father Eusebio Francisco Kino. It was Father Kino who, in 1700,

built the first church, two miles from the present mission, and named it St. Francis Xavier after the Jesuit "Apostle to the Indies."

The present structure was begun in 1783 and took fourteen years to complete. It is acclaimed as the finest example of mission architecture in the United States, a design characterized by late Mexican Renaissance influenced by Moorish and Byzantine architecture. The facade of ornamental detail is flanked by terraced towers; and between the towers, the majestic dome rises.

The exterior was constructed of burned brick and covered with lime plaster, hence the white facade. The walls are three feet thick except those below the towers. Here, because of the tremendous weight, the walls are almost six feet thick.

The architect and builder, Ignacio Gaona, left his stamp of humor on the inside of the church. Carved in full relief on the inner curves of the lower volutes are a cat and a mouse staring at each other across the breadth of wall. The Indians of San Xavier say, "when the cat catches the mouse, the end of the world will come."

Overleaf: "White Dove of the Desert"
H. Armstrong Roberts

51

Houses of Worship Today

"We build for ever . . . let us think, as we lay stone on stone, that a time is to come when those stones will be held sacred because our hands have touched them."

John Ruskin

Today, houses of worship of various denominations stretch across the land. These buildings stand as a visible testimony to America's heritage. They embody the faith and stamina of those first pilgrims and explorers who came to these shores, the patriotic determination and courage of those who dared uphold the novel concept of freedom of religion and that fervor and human compassion which led men of an earlier time to reach out toward new spiritual and physical frontiers.

This unique history, in which freedom and religion coexist, has allowed the construction of cathedrals, temples, and meeting houses side by side, where they exist in harmony of purpose if not in harmony of thought. This heritage has offered a haven in the land and welcomed the religions of the world while allowing new thoughts and creeds to develop and grow.

The churches of today, then, are the culmination of all the work and faith of those men and women long since gone whose only aim was to live their lives in glory to God—and allow their neighbors to do the same.

Original First Church of Christ, Scientist, on right. Extension of First Church on left with dome.

First Church of Christ, Scientist
Boston, Massachusetts

The denomination of Christian Science is an American phenomenon and has its roots in a small frame building in Oconto, Wisconsin, where the first Christian Science services were held. The sect was founded by Mary Baker Eddy. When the building in Oconto became too small and Mrs. Eddy's following so large, she urged the Church directors to erect a "Mother Church."

Work began on this church in 1893; the first service was held on January 6, 1895. An inscription on the wall reads, "The First Church of Christ, Scientist, erected Anno Domini, 1894. A testimonial to our beloved teacher, the Reverend Mary Baker Eddy: Discoverer and Founder of Christian Science; author of its text-book, Science and Health with Key to the Scriptures; President of the Massachusetts Metaphysical College, and the first Pastor of this Denomination."

The church is decorated with stained glass windows and Romanesque architecture. By 1904 the Boston membership had grown large enough to facilitate a new building. The Extension was completed in 1906 and made The First Church the largest church in the city of Boston. At the dedication of this new portion, a message by Mrs. Eddy was read which termed this monumental structure "a magnificent temple wherein to enter and pray."

Temple of Latter Day Saints

Salt Lake City, Utah

The great Temple of Latter Day Saints is the focal point and center of the city of Salt Lake as well as the center of a religion. The site of the Temple was chosen only four days after the Mormons arrived in Utah.

The story is told that Brigham Young was walking with his associates when he suddenly stopped and declared, "Here we will build the Temple of our God." That evening, a ten-acre block was marked for the Temple Square. The city of Salt Lake was planned around this square.

Construction of the Temple began in 1853, even though the people were almost destitute and newly arrived in a strange land. The building and furnishing followed the pattern of the temples of old—only the finest materials were used. One of the crowning treasures, perhaps, is on top of the highest tower where the angel Moroni, from the book of Mormon, stands sculpted of hammered copper and covered with gold leaf.

It was not until April 6, 1892, that the members dedicated the Temple. The day prior to the dedication was open house to non-Mormons. Not since that day have any but Mormons been allowed to enter the Temple.

The Temple was built to last—its walls are from six to nine feet thick. Endurance was what Brigham Young had in mind in the beginning. His desire was to see the Temple "built in a manner that will endure through the Millenium. I want that Temple to stand as a proud monument of the faith, perseverance and industry of the Saints of God in the mountains, in the nineteenth century."

And so it stands.

Mormon Tabernacle

Close to the temple stands the Mormon Tabernacle with its great oval roof resembling, from the air, a great covered dish. The Tabernacle serves as a meeting place for the General Conferences of the Church of Jesus Christ of Latter-Day Saints, and as a cultural center. Musical artists, presidents, and the famous Tabernacle Choir have performed and spoken there.

The Tabernacle set an architectural precedent when construction began September 1, 1865. It took almost two years to complete. The construction was directed by the architect in the tradition of the master builder and from a plan inspired by Brigham Young who had specified a building be raised with no inner columns.

The idea accepted for the Tabernacle was one by former bridge builder Henry Grow. No drawings for the building existed. Grow's scheme was to employ lattice trusses to span a meeting house much as they would support a span across a river. These latticed timbers are fastened together only with large wooden pins. The great roof rests like an inverted bowl on forty-four pillars of sandstone. Each pillar is nine feet from outside to inside the building, three feet thick, and from fourteen to twenty feet high.

Although the Temple is closed to non-Mormons, the Mormon Tabernacle, home of the great choir, is open to all.

Above: Temple Square at Christmastime with Temple's lighted spires. On the left in the picture is the dome of the great Tabernacle. Right: Mormon Tabernacle choir

Riverside Church
New York, New York

H. Armstrong Roberts

58

Entrance to Riverside Church.

Close-up of sculpture at entrance.

Riverside Church in New York City is a nondenominational church whose only requirement for membership is an affirmation of faith in Jesus Christ. This was one of the conditions agreed upon when Harry Emerson Fosdick accepted the pastorate of the old Park Avenue Baptist in 1922. The other condition agreed upon by the church and Fosdick, who was a Presbyterian and a liberal, was a new and larger building. It still stands today, fifty years later.

The architects of Riverside, Charles Collens and Henry C. Pelton, chose as their model one of the most beautiful cathedrals in the world, that of Chartres, France. Beauty played a dominant role in Riverside. Dr. Fosdick spoke of the beauty of the church on the first day the church was opened, Sunday, October 5, 1930. On that day, more than 6,000 people sought admission.

The beauty of the building reflects the liberal theology of its first pastor and creator. The chancel screen portrays St. Luke flanked by Louis Pasteur and Sir Joseph Lister. Christ stands with Socrates, Erasmus and Pestalozzi. The lovely stained glass windows deal with agriculture, government and learning. And carved into the arches of the West Portal are philosophers and scientists including Descartes, Spinoza, Kant, Darwin, Confucius, Buddha, Mohammed and Einstein.

The tower of Riverside houses twenty-two floors of office space and meeting rooms. The belfry houses the seventy-three-bell Laura Spellman Rockefeller Memorial Carillon.

During the depression years, the church became active in social services and began the Social Service Department. Riverside has been successful in this area; and now the beauty of the building blends in a desire to benefit society.

Carmen Johnson

Left: Entrance to Bahá'í House of Worship. Right: Interior of the dome of Bahá'í House of Worship.

Bahá'í House of Worship
Wilmette, Illinois

The Taj Mahal of Chicago. This is what the delicate and filigreed Bahá'í house of worship is often called. The Bahá'í Faith is a relatively new religion, beginning in about the mid-nineteenth century in Persia. By 1920, the national Bahá'í convention in New York was well attended and was considering designs for a Bahá'í house of worship in this country.

A plaster model for the structure was submitted by a French-Canadian architect, Louis J. Bourgeois. The design had taken three years to complete and seemed to be the physical manifestation of the delegate's specifications. A former president of the New York chapter of American Institute of Architects said of the design: "The architect has conceived a Temple of Light in which structure, as usually understood, is to be concealed, visible support eliminated as far as possible, and the whole building to take on the airy fabric of a dream."

The construction of this visible dream began in Wilmette, Illinois, in 1921; but building halted after the foundation was laid. Two problems confronted the Bahá'ís: funds, and the difficulty of translating the model into the large building.

Rising from seven acres of land, the Bahá'í house of worship resembles a great bell. Although the physical structure of the building is unique, Bahá'í teachings require only one tenet for construction: that the Temple have nine sides, with a dome encompassing all.

All people are welcomed into the auditorium for prayer and meditation. Here seats face the Holy Land; and above the heads of worshipers in the apex of the dome is a symbol of the Greatest Name and an invocation to God in Arabic, translated as "O Glory of the All Glorious."

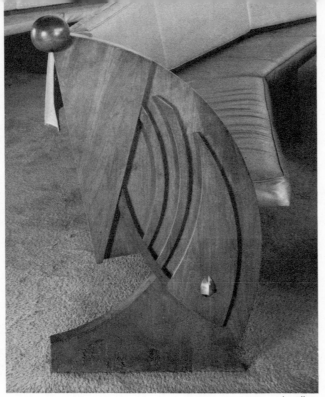

Left: Close-up of pew end in the shape of a fish. Below: The church of the Annunciation is the scene for this wedding. The icon screen is on both sides and above the altar. To the left is one of the free-standing chandeliers.

Greek Orthodox Church of the Annunciation
Milwaukee, Wisconsin

The Greek Orthodox Church of the Annunciation is unique in that it is the last major work of Frank Lloyd Wright, America's most well-known architect. Wright died two years before the building was completed, but the church is his creation from the domed roof to the pews within.

Wright used the rich symbolism of the Greek Orthodox traditions in the design. The basic shape of the building is in the form of the Greek cross; the church proper is circular with only the four arms of the cross breaking the circle. Topping the circular portion is the dome, symbolizing the heavenly home of God. The eaves of the roof form a structure reminiscent of the crown of thorns, an ever-present reminder of the Crucifixion. The blue-tiled dome of the roof presented a structural problem solved by resting the dome on ball bearing-like devices which allow for the expansion and contraction of the concrete.

The nave of the church is also decorated in blue and white. The pews are on increasing levels and curve around to face the pulpit, the icon screen, and the sanctuary behind the screen. Extending the symbolism to include all the details, Wright allowed for pews whose ends resemble the shape of a fish and the three chandeliers represent the Trinity. The chandeliers, however, are not the conventional hanging kind, but rather stand on the floor and point heavenward.

The Church of the Annunciation opens its grounds and doors one weekend each summer with a fair to commemorate the heritage of the Greek people. Greek food and folk dancing are featured as well as tours through one of the most unusual of God's houses, by perhaps America's greatest architect.

St. Patrick's Cathedral
New York, New York

This is the first major cathedral ever to be built in the United States in the Gothic Revival style.

Probably the most famous Catholic church in the United States is St. Patrick's Cathedral. The land for the present cathedral was originally intended for a college. A cathedral was proposed instead, and Archbishop John Hughes instructed the architect James Renwick to prepare designs. The cornerstone was laid in 1858, almost fifty years after the acquisition of the site.

During the Civil War years, construction was halted. It was not until 1879 that the main body of the cathedral was completed. Even then the spires were not raised; that took until 1888.

The cathedral is Gothic and, to some, reminiscent of the cathedrals at Cologne and Rheims.

The foundation is built on solid rock. A natural rock ledge rises nearly to the surface of Fifth Avenue, the street which the cathedral faces. This rock ledge slopes east to about twenty feet below the surface of the south transept.

St. Patrick's exterior is of white marble, and is so well constructed that no cracks have appeared in the walls during the last ninety plus years. The walls are backed by brick and stone and rough masonry with hollow spaces between which prevent dampness and aid ventilation.

Christmas and Easter services are famous and attendance great. Advance tickets are required for Christmas midnight mass and Christmas and Easter Pontifical high mass.

Above: Inside the new St. Louis Cathedral is
the largest collection of mosaics in the world.
Opposite: The Old Cathedral stands framed by
the Gateway to the West Arch.

St. Louis Cathedrals
St. Louis, Missouri

St. Louis is home to two extraordinary
cathedrals. The Old Cathedral of St. Louis
is the oldest cathedral west of the Mississippi River; it was dedicated in 1834. It traces its
church history as far back as 1672 when Father
Marquette visited the city, and to 1749 when the
parish was organized. The site of the cathedral
was set aside by the architect of the original plans
for the city.

The new St. Louis Cathedral was begun in
1903; and it is noteworthy in its own right. Huge
enough to shelter its predecessor in a corner of its
bulk, the exterior is as grand as the interior is
opulent. The great central dome with its cross on
top rises to 227 feet.

Inside the new cathedral is what is believed
to be the largest and most valuable collection of
mosaics in the world. The mosaics are of glass,
covered by a thin gold film. These one-half inch
squares of glass join with stone to produce large
and striking scenes. Experts estimate that more
than one hundred million pieces of glass and
stone create some ten thousand tones of color. In
magnificence and richness, St. Louis Cathedral
has few equals.

St. John the Divine
New York, New York

Work began on the structure of St. John the Divine in New York City in 1892 and continues today. When completed, St. John's will be the largest Gothic cathedral in the world. Its great length includes the majestic west front with five entrances. All entrances lead to the Great Chair, the Sanctuary and the High altar around which are towering columns and the seven chapels and baptistry.

The cathedral was built in the French Gothic Cruciform with the head of the cross facing East. The seven chapels radiate from the apse, or semi-circular eastern end of the choir. The tallest portions of the cathedral are the twin towers on the western front, which rise 266.5 feet, and the central spire, which is 452 feet tall.

The space dimensions of the great cathedral are staggering. It extends for more than one tenth of a mile, is six hundred feet long and three hundred thirty feet across the transepts. It covers an area of 121,000 square feet and seats ten thousand, with standing room for thousands more. This immense structure, however, is built on solid rock; rock which is at some points seventy-two feet below the surface.

The interior of the cathedral contains great works of art, beginning with the great doors. These were an extraordinary achievement by one man. Henry Wilson sculpted the doors, devoting three years to the design. They were, however, his last work. Shortly after completing the final models, he died.

These doors weigh twelve tons and are more than eighteen feet high. Cast in bronze, the principle detail is the sculpture of the panels, each of which contains a scene from the Old and New Testaments.

The Cathedral of St. John the Divine has been called, and truly is, "The Word in Stone."

Below: Model of the completed edifice on display in the cathedral museum.

Air Force Cadet Chapel
Colorado Springs, Colorado

The spires of the Air Force Academy Chapel, like the mountains behind it, reach for the sky. These seventeen silvery spires of the chapel are as modern as the jet-age military it serves, yet reminiscent of Gothic structures long ago. The chapel was designed by Walter A. Netsch of Chicago; the plans took five years to finalize and the construction four years.

The chapel serves the cadets of all faiths, so within the walls are three chapels, for Protestant, Catholic, and Jewish services, as well as a non-denominational meeting room. The kneelers of the chapels were hand-stitched by the wives of the various Air Force officers' wives clubs throughout the world.

On entering the Protestant chapel, one is struck by the multicolored light filtering through

Courtesy United States Air Force Academy

the one-inch thick stained glass. In front of the reredos stands the holy table, and over it a forty-six-inch aluminum cross floats, seemingly appearing and disappearing, depending upon the viewing angle.

The Catholic chapel is accented by a marble sculpture of an abstract representation of the firmament. One figure represents "Our Lady of the Skies" and the other the Guardian Angel. Above the two figures, a dove, symbolic of the Holy Spirit, hovers.

The Jewish chapel is circular in shape, symbolizing the monotheism of the Jewish faith and the global mission of the U.S. Air Force. The foyer floor of this chapel is in Jerusalem brownstone, a donation from the Israeli Defense Forces.

The chapel is, as one writer described it "at once old and new, physical and spiritual, solid and soaring, of the earth and of outer space." It remains a place wherein all cadets can enter and pray, "Lord, guard and guide the men who fly."

Albin E. Kubala

National Cathedral
Washington, D. C.

Rising from fifty-seven acres of land, the Cathedral of St. Peter and St. Paul joins other national treasures of the Washington skyline. The cathedral is the materialization of a wish first voiced by President Washington, that this nation have a great church for all the people—a National Cathedral.

In 1893, the Congress of the United States granted a group of laymen the Charter of the Washington Cathedral. This charter provided a "House of Prayer for all people, forever free and open, welcoming all who enter its doors." The cornerstone of the great cathedral was laid in 1907; and the Bethlehem chapel, the first chapel to be completed, was finished in 1910.

The physical plan of the Cathedral is as grand in design as is its charter. The present schedule calls for the completion of the towers, the final phase, in 1980. Those towers will rise 107 feet above the Washington Monument. The gothic cathedral spreads over one tenth of a mile and ranks sixth in the world in area (75,000 square feet). Construction experts believe the building will last 3,000 years.

In keeping with the charter which specifies a cathedral "for all people," five denominations use the building regularly: the Protestant Episcopal (which holds the charter), Russian Orthodox, Temple Sinai Jewish Congregation, Polish National Catholic, and St. Andrew's Ukrainian Orthodox. In keeping with its national design, each Sunday the cathedral honors a state by special prayers for the people of that state.

Throughout, the cathedral mingles Biblical figures and national scenes. The parables and miracles of Christ are depicted in stained glass as are the lives of Generals Robert E. Lee and Stonewall Jackson. Needlework throughout the cathedral was done by women from all over the country. The kneelers in the Children's Chapel depict animals and Noah's Ark. In the War Memorial Chapel, is a huge tapestry containing the seals of all the fifty states and of the five military services. The kneelers in this chapel were worked by English women in gratitude for American help during World War II. One kneeler was even worked by the Queen Mother Elizabeth.

Heroic statues, breathtaking stained glass, and rare books and paintings are housed in the Cathedral. The building is huge, beautiful, and an architectural marvel. The purpose of the National Cathedral, however, transcends these physical treasures. As Francis B. Sayre, Jr., Dean of the Cathedral expresses the purpose: *"Everything accomplished here is done to the glory of God and in gratitude for his many gifts to us. Daily we sing his praises in worship; sometimes our chorus is a thousand voices strong, at other times there may be only two or three. We come to lay our problems, our needs and hopes before him, asking God for strength, and courage enough to do his will. His alone!"*

Morton Broffn

"The greatest glory of a building is not in its stones, or in its gold. Its glory is in its Age."

John Ruskin

A Haven Still

America was settled, for the most part, by Europeans seeking religious refuge. Most of these were Western Europeans. It, therefore, seems fitting somehow that two houses of worship have made their way to America from Europe. It is, perhaps, symbolic of America's commitment to religious freedom that those two churches have been transplanted from the two countries which have figured so prominently in North America's early exploration and settlement—France and England.

Joan of Arc Chapel
Milwaukee, Wisconsin

The Chapelle de St. Martin de Sayssuel was probably built in the fifteenth century, or even before. It was most likely used for devotions and for burials of the elite of the community. Today, however, it stands on the campus of a Midwestern university and is a popular setting for student weddings.

After the French Revolution, the Chapelle de St. Martin fell into disuse and ruin until in 1926 it was acquired by Gertrude Hill Gavin. A year later, the chapel was dismantled and bound for Long Island. There, it was re-erected stone by stone next to a French Renaissance chateau that had also been shipped from France. The chateau later burned, and the chapel was presented to Marquette University in 1964.

To dismantle the chapel, workmen worked for nine months, marking each stone green for the top, red for its bottom, and numbering it inside as to its relation to the others. The stones were then trucked to Milwaukee. Reconstruction began in July 1965. Only small changes were made in the chapel to adapt it to the campus. For instance, the nave was lengthened, necessitating the addition of several windows.

The Chapelle de St. Martin de Sayssuel was dedicated to Joan of Arc, its most revered treasure being the famous Joan of Arc stone. Legend says that Joan of Arc prayed before a statue of Our Lady which was standing on this stone. As Joan ended her prayer, she kissed the stone which has ever since remained colder than those around it. It now rests in a niche of the chapel.

St. Mary, Aldermanbury

Fulton, Missouri

For almost three centuries, the Church of St. Mary, Aldermanbury, stood on the corner of London's Aldermanbury and Love Lane. Here, in 1656, John Milton married Catherine Woodcock; and most believe that William Shakespeare came the short distance from his home to worship here.

On December 29, 1940, however, an incendiary bomb reduced the structure to rubble. Today, the church has been rebuilt and again stands on a corner; however, the present site is at Westminster Avenue and West Seventh Street on the campus of Westminster College, Fulton, Missouri.

The church is in America as a memorial to Winston Churchill since it was on the Westminster Campus that Sir Winston made a speech at the request of then President Harry Truman. In that speech, delivered on March 5, 1946, Churchill used the now familiar phrase, "an iron curtain has now descended across the continent of Europe." The reconstruction of St. Mary, Aldermanbury, is a fitting tribute to the man who symbolizes the strength and unity of the free world.

The church of St. Mary, Aldermanbury, was designed by Sir Christopher Wren—perhaps one of England's greatest architects. Today it is as it was on its completion in 1677. Leading to the belfry are twenty-seven circular steps; twenty-four of which are from the original church built between the eleventh and twelfth centuries. These steps are all that are left of that church after the Great Fire of London.

To reconstruct the church, seven hundred tons of stone were shipped across the Atlantic. Each stone was scrubbed and numbered. Once in Missouri, the stones were reassembled on top of a museum and library of Churchill memorabilia. To retain authenticity, the new stones necessary to replace those destroyed by the bombing were quarried from the mine which furnished the original stone.

Because the church was damaged by a Zeppelin bomb in World War I and gutted by an incendiary bomb in the blitz of London, 1940, President Kennedy wrote of the church:

"It will tie together powerful events—the 17th century, 1940 and the blitz, the Iron Curtain address and the extraordinary and powerful influence on the free world of Sir Winston Churchill's public service."

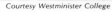

Left: The organ in the choir loft is a modern tracker type instrument built by Noel P. Mander Ltd. of London. The case was originally built in 1741 for the organ in Woolwich Parish Church, Kent, England. Right: The ruins that remained after an incendiary bomb struck the church on the night of December 29, 1940. Below: St. Mary, Aldermanbury, stands restored in mid-Missouri as the centerpoint of the Winston Churchill Memorial and Library.

Courtesy Westminister College

Courtesy Westminster College

Glossary

APSE   The round or polygonal termination of the sanctuary of a church.

BASILICA   A Roman Catholic church or cathedral having certain liturgical privileges.

BUTTRESSES   A projecting structure of masonry or wood for support of a wall or holding.

CAMPANILE   A bell tower.

CHANCEL   The part of a church containing the altar or communion table, pulpit, lecturn and usually the choir.

CHAPEL ROYAL   The official place of worship of the British governor of the colony.

CRUCIFORM   A church laid out in the form of a cross.

NAVE   The body of the church building in which the congregation sits; derived from the Latin word "navis," meaning ship, because of the resemblance between the roof inside and an inverted hull.

PALLADIAN WINDOW   A window consisting of a central window with an arched head and on each side a narrower window with a square head.

PORTICO   A colonnade or covered walk, usually at the entrance to a building.

RING, PEAL OR CHIME   A set of bells.

SANCTUARY   The part of a Christian church where general worship services are held.

TRANSEPT   When churches are built in the form of a cross, they have two arms, one on each side of the nave; these are called transepts, north and south.

VAULT   An arched structure of masonary forming a ceiling or roof.

VOLUTE   A spiral or scroll-shaped ornament that forms the chief feature of the Ionic capital.